MR. MICHAEL PRESENTS THE FIVE "S"

EXPRESSIONS OF LOVE FOR MY WIFE AND SPIRITUAL SECRETS OF LIFE

iUniverse, Inc.
Bloomington

Mr. Michael Presents the Five "S"
Expressions of Love for My Wife and Spiritual Secrets of Life

iUniverse books may be ordered through booksellers or by contacting:

iUniverse
1663 Liberty Drive
Bloomington, IN 47403
www.iuniverse.com
1-800-Authors (1-800-288-4677)

Because of the dynamic nature of the Internet, any Web addresses or links contained in this book may have changed since publication and may no longer be valid. The views expressed in this work are solely those of the author and do not necessarily reflect the views of the publisher, and the publisher hereby disclaims any responsibility for them.

ISBN: 978-1-4502-7061-8 (sc)
ISBN: 978-1-4502-7062-5 (ebook)
ISBN: 978-1-4502-7063-2 (hc)

Printed in the United States of America

iUniverse rev. date: 2/02/2011

Contents

DEDICATION

I DEDICATE THIS BOOK OF LOVE AND KNOWLEDGE

TO MY WIFE, "MS. C"

ACKNOWLEDGMENT

You have a knowledge that there's a power greater than you; one who created all within you. Take a moment and look around yourself, of the million-billion-trillions of life giving gifts that are free to us all, so that our bodies can exist on it's on merits, we have air, water, sunlight, and night to rest to restore one's body.

Body - a word that truly means life in which we are able to live, touch, smell, taste and feel pain, to have the ability and the knowledge to learn, to grow your own foods, a knowledge of the wide span between right and wrong, good and evil.

Through it all, the earth on it's own turns and seasons change without any help from man. Morning always follows nights. No matter if it's a very cloudy day, the sun is always shining. Given these truths, we are not an accident or just a bad experiment by a mad scientist.

Give acknowledgment of our existence by God, a higher power, or whosoever you want to give thanks to. With this knowing you have unlimited ability and power but first you must recuperate from your lack of knowledge.

When you accept that there are so many levels of knowledge that one can reach, each new level of learning about who you are, who you can become, and the many goals and levels there are for us to reach is unlimited.

Thus, this puts us beyond our human bodies. Now, we are speaking in a spiritual realm! You always must seek wisdom, knowledge, and understanding of the vast spaces within us and all around us. When you start seeking wisdom, which is the breath of God, knowledge is knowing how and when we use this power and yes, it is power. Power that is more powerful than ever man can imagine. The understanding is the inner spirit of God's heart. As God said, "I made man and I saw that man was alone. So I cast a deep sleep over him." A s man lay down in a deep sleep, God removed a bone from his rib. With that bone, God created woman. Woman is from the body of man, so in order for man to be complete, he must be joined together with his missing bone!!

When a man has the right woman in his life, he then becomes the being that God first created!

People waste many lifetimes, take many wrong turns, searching, studying, trying everything they can under the sun for answers to things they don't even know the questions to.

If we would only take just a moment alone with God and just be still and just listen, listen from within, and put aside all the book learned knowledge and life learned lessons, then we will see the acidulous people that we allow to influence our lives.

When the student is ready the teacher will appear! This statement is repeated by my wife all the time and the meaning is very grounded with her wisdom! Just by listening to nature, allowing your heart to speak to your soul and find people who are spiritual in their own right, you will know them, when they are among you.

They have a light that shines in their eyes, their smiles are luminous, also even when they are walking, if you look at them from within your soul, you can see the "spirit of energy" walking with them. I said these truths are of my own life learned lessons, and with this knowledge of who God is within me. I also have learned that the words from my mouth are more powerful than any sword. So when I speak, I must always speak of the truth and righteousness, and never have any bad feelings toward any human being!

Because these words can come true and put things from my lips into action, again I am only passing on to you some of my own life learned lessons. We are all here with alienable rights of life learned lessons. For me the worst one can do is to not share this knowledge with the world. These lessons are your seeds to plant, not just a man's sperm or a woman's eggs!

RESOURCEFULNESS - RESPONSIBILITY - OWN UP TO THEM!

You are responsible for the choices you make in your own life and others also. Whether you know or admit it, we all are responsible for each other. So given the resources all around us we must master making the best of choices over all; not just for oneself or just for your family, or your "kind", but for the world. No matter how large or how small, we are all one people; one race -the human race; under God, in his mercy and under his will. So a good seed grows good choices.

A bad selfish seed damages us all. in order for me to go farther, all I am saying up until this point is to open your hearts first, then we can deal with your mind. You must be willing to accept that you are not as smart as you think you are; even myself. It really just comes down to how smart we think we are! You must look at yourself as an outsider would look at you.

Ask questions about yourself, but make sure these questions are true hard hitting fact finding questions. in other words, ask yourself the truth about your life and where you need to go right now.

What do I need to find my true self? First, you must learn to love yourself, not to be in love with yourself. There's a difference between the two, like day and night. When you love yourself you learn to love others, and the world around you and you will not allow someone else to mistreat you or be mean to anyone else. When you are in love with yourself, you are narrow and self centered. These thoughts and opinions are just that, my thoughts and my opinions. I am not forcing them on anyone.

CHAPTER ONE: FIRST "S" SPECIAL

YOUR WIFE - YOUR WOMAN - YOUR PARTNER - OR YOUR TRUE LOVE!

In my life, when I married my soul mate, everyday is as follows: whenever I walk into a room full of people and my wife is there, before I do or say anything, I go to her first and greet her with hugs and kisses, conversation, and only then do I converse with everyone else, if I need to. No matter how many people are present she is never far from my arms reach or my eyesight, nor is the sound of her voice. When we are about to sit down at a table I will pull her chair out for her and make sure she is comfortable. If and when she rises from her seat, I stand and pull her chair out for her and wait patiently for her return to her seat, to hold her chair for her again. I also place her food order and/or her beverages.

Whenever we are entering a building, house, car, etc., I open every door for her and close every door behind her. My wife and I have certain code words, meaning if we are at a function and one of us says the word "dyn_____", this means to stop and leave right now. The next code words are "el_____ has left the building," meaning in three minutes, we must leave.

If we are talking on the phone, there are code words we use to alert each other that there is eminent trouble. My wife is not my servant.

We cook and clean our home together as husband and wife as a team. There are times I will cook for us. I love cooking! There are many times I will call her while I am on my way home from work or just coming home. I will call her to tell her not to cook because I will bring something home with me, or, take her out to eat. I can't tell you how many times I am out and about when I see couples together, walking to their car, and the man never opens the car door for his woman. Most men jump in first then push a button so that his woman is waiting for their car door to unlock, and that she can open the door to get in herself. This is sad and shows no respect for his woman from him.

So many times after grocery shopping, couples will get to their car, and the first thing the man should do is open the door for his woman so that she is safe inside the car; then, start to put their groceries in the car, but time after time, most men will leave their woman standing outside the car while he loads the groceries. Then he gets in the car and pushes that unlock button so that his woman can get in the car herself. These men are "do-do heads!!'"".

When entering any building, I open all doors for my wife. Entering any elevator, she steps in first. This also goes for any door; she steps in first, and always before me.

Every month, every second weekend, when my wife has to work, I will go to the farmers market where I can buy individual flowers and fillers. I buy four dozen long stem roses, 70cm. I also arrange them myself (with so much love) and after twenty years I have become very good at my arrangements. I have only missed one weekend not buying her roses. All of her customers call my wife the "rose lady". There are so many of her customers that come by just to see the roses. These roses never speak a word, but mean so much not only to my wife, but to so many other people.

No matter where I am or how long my day was, or what I may be doing, I make sure I am at her job when she is closing up at work, I am always there every night.

Making sure she gets to her car safe, I will then follow her from work in my car every night, no exceptions. I am there for her until we both pull up to our home, and we are both safe inside. When my wife and I are just walking anywhere, my wife is on the inside of our walk, and I am on the outside. I see so many couples walking along the streets or in the malls, and the male is walking on the inside and the female is walking on the outside, where there is more danger for her. Once again this shows no respect for this woman and another case of "do-do head males". Even if after a long day, when I get home, this is not a reason for an excuse for not giving my wife all of me, whether this means running bath water for her, giving her a bath, rubbing her feet or back, or just listening to how was her day. "Listening" to her is very important. I already know about my day! Because her opinion is very valuable to me in this marriage, we are as one, we both are equal.

CHAPTER TWO: COMPROMISE!

In most relationships, people feel in order to be as one you have to compromise; meaning you must give up something in order to get along.

But in my relationship with my wife, neither one of us had to compromise anything or lose anything in our lives. There is enough time and room we give to each other so that we only add to each other! It is the sharing and giving to our relationship. You should never have to give up anything just to be in a relationship. No matter when or where my wife and I go, when we are riding in the car the radio is very low and we talk while we are riding to our destination. Once we leave the car, after I always again and again open the door for her, we start walking as we always do and hold hands or she holds on to my arm.

I am my wife's rock and she is my anchor. If I am shopping with my wife, I never rush her on her shopping time. I also at the beginning of each spring, take my wife on a shoe shopping hunt for the new spring shoes!

When I look around at the other couples, they are like two strangers toward each other. They are never holding hands as they walk apart, or setting at a table eating together never talking to each other. While driving at certain times I look in my rearview mirror only to see the couple in the car behind us are not talking to each other.

The woman is sitting so far apart from her male companion it looks like she is sitting on her door! I sometimes even look at couples `walking down the street and they seem to be forcing themselves to be with each other. I could never imagine not holding my wife's hand as we are walking anywhere. There were many times when my so called boys wanted to hang out, and my answer was "I am going home!" They just laugh and call me henpecked. All I can say to them is "as long as it's by the right hen, then I guess I am henpecked!!!"

At this period in my life, I knew then that my "boys" were not good for me and the price of their friendship was too costly. So now, I only have seven true friends in the world; my wife and the other six are all on the face of green paper.

Their names are as follows: Franklin- $100 bill, Grant- $50 bill, Jackson-$20 bill, Hamilton-$10 bill, Lincoln-$5 bill, and Washington-$1 bill. These are my new homeboys! They never let me down, never laugh at me nor leave me hanging. Always there for me when I say let's roll, they roll right with me.

Because of the way I look, dress, talk, and body shape, most other men are insecure when they are around me with their women. Their insecurity shows more openly as though they have to mark their "property" by kissing their women, or even worse, groping her! What a shame! Yes, I have a witness - my wife. My wife!! This word wife has a strong meaning. She is not just a relationship but is a very important part of you that you can't put a price on her! There have been times I lay awake at night and can't go back to sleep because of my workday or other matters regarding who or what would control my day.

Each time, at that exact moment, my wife reaches over and holds my hand, or caresses her foot with my foot. With her touch it tells me that don't worry my love, everything is going to be alright and she has my back.

She allows me to be me and I don't have to be superman. I can just be her man. I have never felt so free by being with one person I can make mistakes and her eyes are telling me, "Yes my love, you can make mistakes because you are human." I can show my emotions when my eyes fill with water and still this is "ok"!

I enjoy cooking and cleaning our home. I enjoy washing dishes or whatever we do in our home, because we do it together. No one says they're tired of doing all the work around this house. Reason is, we live in this house together, so together we make this house 'our home!'

There's never a day when I don't have time or am too tired for my wife, when she is in need of my "famous" back rub, then the rub is on! When she is lying across my lap and I am rubbing her back, the love my hands feel from this touching no words could ever express this fullness. When she says you can stop when you get tired, she slowly goes off to sleep.

I know that her trust in me is so strong that she can go to sleep knowing I am there with her. There's not a time I can think about not being with her or I am not in her life. No matter how much money I have, without her I could not enjoy this wealth. We have the best bed on the market. The moment I lay down on our bed, within five minutes, I am dead sleep, because my wife is next to me. But if for some other reason she is not there with me, and I lay down, no matter how tired I might be, I can't go to sleep because my wife is this bone that God has put in my life, and that is why I am the man I am today.

There's no question about this matter. My wife is a very strong minded and willed woman. She can do very well without me, but she opened up her life and allowed me to live in her world and now, her world and my world have become "our world!" I owe my success to my wife. When I was running low on myself, she stood up and lifted me up.

She was always there to push me down the road even when I couldn't go any farther myself. When I have thoughts of her I regain my second wind! There have been many days I was sick or hurting, but I still got up and went to work because I couldn't give up on us.

Every day I will say the 23rd psalm and it will give me the strength to continue through my day!

The peace of God fills my spirit and I give thanks everyday for my blessings and my wonderful gifts in the human form of my wife, because God and only God could have created this woman for me. There have been many times when we were out and about travelling in the city and people would just stare at us or just start talking as if they knew us. There was this particular moment catching a flight and we were checking our bags with a skycap. We were just being ourselves and at that exact moment the skycap said to us "you guys must have just got married because you are too happy".

Most couples he said he encounters everyday are fighting, arguing, or standing far apart from each other. "Sometimes they never ever talk to each other so you must be newlyweds". We laughed and answered him by saying, "we have been married for 25 years, and you have a very nice day". Another time we were in the mall waiting for the elevator, when the doors opened and a young lady exited while we were getting on. She turned and looked at us to say, " You two look so very happy together" and we said "we are and thank you".

I recall the first time I saw her. I was on my way to work one night and I stopped at this Revco (now CVS) to make a purchase of some breath mints. As I was standing in line at the front of the store to pay for the mints, my eyes were drawn upward to the back of the store to this most beautiful woman I have ever set my eyes on. Emotions were moving inside of me and for the first time in my life, I was spellbound and at a loss for words! So I went on my way, but as I began my night, I could not get her out of my thoughts; thoughts I never knew I had.

Notice I have worked in the nightclub business for over twenty years. So I have seen all the "t & a" any man could see in twenty life times and therefore women were not my weakness. But the next night, I found myself standing in line again at the Revco, looking at "her" again, and after the fifth night (shameful), I said enough is enough. I must meet her.

So the next day I had a prescription for athlete's feet and I went back to the pharmacy. Being that "she" was the pharmacist, I gave her assistant my prescription and waited for it. At this time I introduced myself to "her" and she in return introduced herself. She finally became more than just a beautiful face, but a voice that even today is still the most beautiful sound I have ever heard! So after other excuses and reasons I found myself back in Revco again and again.

We started dating and the rest is 38 years later. I have never had any regrets!! Let my wife tell her side of our meeting, she tells everyone I was stalking her, and this is why this is "Special".

Know this-life is life: as though the world turns from night to day to the four seasons is the reason for our lives. Ask many questions of why? What am I going to do while I am here? Why am I not happy or why I don't enjoy things as I once did? One must understand as we grow older and wiser, our desires change along with our wants and needs. Let's first examine ourselves before we can ask of others to fulfill our needs. Where are you in life at this moment?

Who are you at this time in your life? Do you know where you are going and how are you going to get there? What are your plans & do you know what you need to get there? Questions about you by you every day! Many people spend many years in higher learning, having many titles in front of their names, and many letters behind their names, and we are still feeling empty. All of these achievements/accomplishments are nothing but fillers from life and when we look at our accomplished lives we still are not full. Reason being these achievements are all manmade and what men overlook is everything manmade soon fades away.

Spiritual secrets for me are my answers. They were here before man and are here for man, that which will sustain him through this life and even beyond, but this spiritual secret will come up later in another chapter!

Socialites - family and friends tell us all how to live, who we should be, how we must look, and pick the right people we live and play with. If at any moment in your life you go against these demons, these people who can't even control their own lives, they get angry. We look through this telescope of life looking for the perfect fit in life so that we can live happily ever after.

But what we don't realize is we first must clean out ourselves, of all doubts, all fears, insecurities, and all of the bad people in our lives. First ourselves! So when the right person comes along, you will know who they are.

They will come from every walk of life also! Because a person swept streets for a living is not the full measure of that person. Most people are always looking in all the wrong places, and never find their true being.

When a person extends themselves beyond what we ask of them, it let's you see this person's true being. When a man places all of his energy into his family, when he turns off the television on the weekends from sports, he tunes into his wife, or woman, and family. Spending warm close moments with them and making a home with them. A place when you need support. A place of love and strength, that only grows, and grows. When a man expresses himself in a loving way his actions will speak loudly and boldly for him and leave no doubts about his meaning. His home goes head first on his day from home, helping him face whatever comes his way because his home gives him his strength. Again, here's this secret energy!

When a man finds his true love, there's nothing or no one in this world that could or would change this love! He will never risk this great lost. Even until the point of dying for or risking his life and limbs. A man's wife is everything (first) to him, not his children, not his monies, cars or boats. What he wants for his woman is to help her grow, grow into the full being of her ability, growing day by day. Her growth is the full test of his love.

In return, she will help him grow by her love for him, which she gives to him in the many ways only she can give. His strength becomes her strength and as nature designs, all their love grows, and grows for the world to see. This is one of God's main gifts to this world. Once a woman realizes with this man is her strength, there's nothing she and he can't do or even have. Understanding a marriage is a work in progress, meaning everyday you must work on it, not only to make it bigger, but better.

You both must nurture your marriage "every day". Give respect toward each other. The more we put in, the more our love and marriage will grow. If your man is not pulling his own weight and always giving you excuse after excuse, what he is telling you is that you are in the relationship all by yourself, and he is just going along for the free ride! So don't waste your life with this "do-do head", because "do-do heads" never change, and the same goes for a "pepper head" (woman).

People must understand you can't change anyone at a point in their adult life. This person is who they are and their actions will let you know who they are.

The most precious thing you have in this life is the time you are given here in this world. No one is here to be a slave or servant to anyone. A woman is not second to man and supposed to service only him at his order of his mind. Run as fast as you can away from this man, because love is not in this man's life for you, and likewise, for any man in which a woman needs him as her servant. It takes two people always together as a team hand and hand in a joint venture living and sharing each other together with one purpose; our happiness together as one! My love for my wife is never living a day without her.

When I look into my wife's eyes, all I see is an outpouring of love for me. There's nothing, or no one that can force or make me hurt or harm her. There will never come a time when my wife has any regrets about her decision to marry me.

When a woman is in love, no matter where she goes, when you look into her eyes they sparkle, her smile is luminous, and her happiness is all over her.

When a man cheats on his woman, not only does he break his trust and his wife's heart, he could never remove the hurt. Also, he has destroyed her trust in him. When a woman is having an affair with the knowledge this man is married, she is a destroyer of trust. Also, this is a selfish act from the two of them. Please ladies, if this happens to you, here's what you must do for yourself: run - run; run as fast and as far away from him as you can because this man is no longer the man you fell in love with and married.

Because once trust is broken, it will never be the same and all is left are lies and more lies and you deserve more for yourself. This is also true for any man with a cheating wife! Run - run - run as fast and as far away as you can, please!

Now, don't misread me, because I am in my early 60's and have shoulder length wavy hair, and at the end it curls into smaller curls. I'm 5'11 and 205 lbs. My waist line is 33 inches, my chest 50 inches, which is a body that makes a 30 year old backup and take a second look. Oh, also my eyes are green/golden, and my coolness is so true that when I worked in the nightclubs, I was given the name "Rico Suave".

If I wanted to go farther, 98% of the women in the world, yes I said world, I could have my choice. The other 2% are only the ones that are married or too young or too old. By having 98% of women, does not mean getting them in bed! No, my meaning is getting to know them as themselves, becoming their friend, having a true friendship with no sex as a part of our friendship. Yes, men and women can be friends without having sex!!

Please don't misunderstand my meaning about myself, as if I'm saying I am all that and more. No sir, I have gone through the school of hard knocks by women. I have been a fool over a woman, a fool for a woman, been skinned up by a woman, had my head bumped by a woman! My mother once called me a 'green apple' oh yeah!

But because of the many lessons from women and my experiences from the night clubs, I have mastered the art of women, drugs, alcohol, and money. All men must achieve these levels of mastery in order to truly reach a high level of spiritual being of their true selves! It's alright to enjoy the many pleasures of life but please, keep yourself safe and only do things in moderation! But I get attention wherever I go.

The attention I love the most is the attention I get from my wife when we are together. So I am not out of shape or hard on the eyes, as I have heard so many times, he's a "keeper!" I want the world to know how much I love my wife. I would kill a rock to protect my wife. I say to any person, don't stay in a bad relationship, why when there are six and one-half billion people in the world!

There have only been maybe six arguments between my wife and me, and I started all of them, but the last, and I mean last one, was when I saw the hurt in my wife's face; that was it! Never again will I let my own "do-do head" out, and that day he died!! I see so many beautiful women in the world filled with so much love, but there is no one there for them to give this love to.

So a lot of women settle for less just to say they have a piece of a man. You don't have to settle for less. Never sell yourself short! Having the love of my life is a piece of heaven on earth.

This is my only way to express to you our love by telling our story. Hopefully, this will help people to open their minds. Please!!!

CHAPTER THREE: SECOND "S" - SECURITY

By freeing her mind of any doubts about her safety, giving her the total freedom of being herself, supporting her a thousand and one percent, I watch her grow into the beautiful being she truly is inside. I make sure that she knows that I will always be there for her and the full unwavering love for her from me. The security of our finances is that before I die she will never have a lack of money and always live the lifestyle she is accustomed to.

No matter where we are or where we go her protection is my first action. The whole world will know how much love I have for her and the strength of my protection. Her growth is key to her being in total control of her own life, being able to choose and have free will of her own mind.

In return, my security is also strengthened from her love and the stronger she is, the stronger we are together. A man must be willing to give any and everything for the protection of his wife, and I pointedly say his wife. Even to die for her in order to protect her. Every man must die, but only a few men will truly live life to it's fullness.

I will be using every effort to put attention and love in her true being. By helping her to be comfortable and safe in her own skin, with the knowledge that even when we are apart, she can feel the strength of my security and my strength for her, that with her thoughts of a need for me, I will be there always for her.

COMMUNICATION:

Giving her my attention and listening to her at all times, because she has my confidence. It's unanimous when we make decisions on our lives, money, and other choices. Replenish the love of our marriage. Illuminate to the world my love for her and our unity. Together as one, two people thinking so much alike, as if we could read each other's thoughts, feel each other's feelings before the other one could speak, we would speak for them.

Our years together represent a long and full life of loving each other. One of our favorite songs is, "I promise" by the Temptations, a very meaningful worded song that you should listen to.

CHAPTER FOUR: STANDING ON THE OUTSIDE

When you are standing on the outside, you should question people on their actions and hold them to their words. Why? A friend is a love for what is best for someone. No matter what, they never have to say "I'm sorry", because you know their words and actions are from the part of them where only love is there for you.

Observe a man by just standing on the outside, such as when the two of you are just walking down the street. Notice his actions, for instance, if his next step will be a life or death situation. There's an ant, and if he takes his next step he will step on that ant and it will die, or will he stop and turn his step so that he will overstep the ant? The two of you are riding down the street and a snake is in the middle of the road. What would be his next act? Will he run over the snake, or just turn to miss it, or just stop the car if he can? You see by standing on the outside and watching his actions about life, his actions will tell you all you need to know about this man's character. A man can be strong but not forceful with his demands, strong but gentle with his emotions. A person must always put forward their best effort to do their best work. Just because one can take advantage of someone or something, we must make the best choices because our actions will be the determining factor for the rest of our lives. It takes more effort to frown and less to smile.

Also, I must say this: most women are emotional beings, but, and I mean but, when you become "Ms. Attitude", thinking this is going to make people act the way you would want them to act or be, "Ms. Attitude" acts as if the world must give into her! This mindset will destroy any relationship, or she feels the world owes "Ms. Attitude" something. When I see her it is a complete turnoff, even when she is by herself, I still see an asshole. Get rid of this deadweight in your life!

Just by being your beautiful self is all you need and the world will get your point. But as long as you live with "Ms. Attitude", you will just about end up by your damn self, and that's where you need to be!

Most women think they can change a man; just listen to this; " I will make him into the man I want him to be!!" This is just all wrong in so many ways!

CHAPTER FIVE: THE FROZEN SNAKE SYNDROME

The frozen snake syndrome! On a very cold, cold evening in the middle of winter, a young woman was walking home back from her evening run, when she stopped and noticed something lying across the pathway of her walk. With shock and dismay, she realized here is a beautiful snake! At this moment she thought the poor snake was dead, but to her surprise the snake moved. Being the compassionate person she was, she picked up the half dead, half frozen creature and carried it back to her home, and started to give life back into the snake by placing it in front of her fireplace to warm it.

She gave it food so that it could regain it's strength. She cared for this creature for months. Then as the snake regained itself, on one long night, this passionate woman was lying in the bed, relaxing from a long day after work. Sometime in the early part of the morning, this snake crawled into the bed where his savior was sleeping, and he bit her.

The pain of his bite was so great, that the woman rolled over and got up out of bed. At this time, she looked back at the bed, to see that the snake was in her bed. Now terror came all over her, and she then asked the snake, "after I saved you from a frozen death, and brought you into my home to give you a home, how and why would you bite me knowing that your bite would kill me?"

Right then, the snake replied, "It's just my nature", and at that exact moment, the woman died from his bite. No matter what, always remember one thing if you don't remember anything else. If and when you meet someone, by chance if they are eating with their hands and feet, why in the hell and who the hell are you to change them? It's their nature, and maybe you could just make sure before they eat with their hands and feet, that they are simply cleaned! You need to work on 'yourself' , look in the mirror at yourself, and ask are you in fact perfect? There's so many thoughts running through my mind, so as they come, I must write them down.

Please-please ladies, when holidays come up, don't lock down your spouse by dragging them down or over to your parents or mother's house, every year after year; or have your husband dragging you kicking/yelling down to his parents/mother's house every year, because we all must understand one thing.

When you get married, your spouse's happiness is a very important part of your marriage and everyone else "must" get in line. This is one surefire spouse killer over the years, putting everyone/everything before your spouse.

Ladies, when you are trying so hard to change your man, the changes you are making are in you. You then stop being his wife and become his mother. So guess what happens to the love for his wife? It becomes a love for his mother. A man must understand his mainstay of security for his wife is to protect her from even his own vices. When a man is out with his wife, the worst and most disrespectful thing a man can do is eyeball all the eye candy all around him. Most men don't even understand that his woman "knows" when a woman, and what kind of woman, would make him turn his head and take a look!

A marriage is a (seal) relationship that the two people involved must work together every day to make it first work, then grow, blossom and enhance your love for each other!! When you're married, the single language is over for you, and now you must go from me, mine, myself and I, to us, we, and my husband and I, or my wife and I, table for two, plans for two!!

CHAPTER SIX: MONSTER INSIDE

This person that exists within you must not ever, never be allowed out. There's no reason in the world for your love ones to live with this monster within; afraid to say or do anything around you that will cause the monster to come out and bring terror in their lives.

They should not have to walk around their home as if walking on eggshells, because of the fear of this monster inside you. Being perfect, as I tried to be for so long, many years raising the bar so high even I couldn't reach it, but expecting everyone else to do so, I was never wrong and everything had to go my way and everyone else was wrong.

Well, Mr./Mrs./Ms. perfect, all you are doing is pushing everyone that loves you away, and making their lives a living hell! With you being "perfect" is boring anyway. Now that I have come to my senses, I enjoy my family more and have so much fun! I can even see the love in their eyes and hear the joy in their voices.

Make damn sure when you are wrong, you apologize to them. Never stop talking to your spouse or get mad or stay angry at them. Never!!!

Arguing is like a (virus) that only poisons the relationship, causes Illness, and death to any marriage. Please stop if you are arguing often and don't start if you're not. Understand each other with respect and love, so no one is right or wrong. Please remember, you love each other. Remembering this first, then you will remember never to argue with your love ones, nor anyone else, because you never have to prove yourself to anyone "but yourself".

CHAPTER SEVEN: THIRD "S" - SHARING

The true nature of sharing yourself with your spouse and your family means an open door for them. My wife is my life, and I have so much extra room in my life for her, that "she" brings more into "my" life. We are partners in every sense. Every dime is 50/50, no matter where life leads us. It will be my final act in this world whether we are married or not, that I will be making sure that she will never have a need for money as well as be able to live her life as she so chooses!

In my daily activities, I ask for her Ideas and her opinions. No secrets when I am on the go; my wife is right there with me. I share all of my Ideas, dreams, and opinions. We are business partners.

When we share with each other we both receive more out of life rather than being separate. We are better together by sharing our emotions and by allowing your spouse to see your weaker side. Sharing paying the bills, sharing monies, housework, etc, are some of the most important qualities of a good relationship.

CHAPTER EIGHT: FREE
WILL AND PATIENCE

**THE FOLLOWING ARE MY OWN
OPINIONS AND LIFE EXPERIENCES.**

All my life I was taught and preached to, that God gave man a free will. But for me, I felt empty and there was always something missing. As I started to gain knowledge from self teaching, I began searching for answers to questions in a spiritual response, and not from man!

Doing a deep spiritual breathing meditation to think deeply, I began to learn the true meaning of "free will" for me. Questions to you: have you ever thought of a person and that same person walked right up in front of you? Have you ever had someone on your mind and that person called you and said that you were on their mind? This is free will. The ability to will the energy around you into action. By you making the connection with this energy that exist here just for us, is God's will! We try so hard to find God, that we look in all the empty spaces from second hand religion that has been past down to us all! We take the wrong information from very toxic people.

We are so eager to be misinformed and lead by a person of the cloth. God gave birds the knowledge how to live without going to any school, and insects make a great go at life too!

Please note! Please people, don't let five minutes of pleasure cause you a lifetime of hell!!

But you must first understand that you can't get or have everything you want or need just by thinking . And like Aladdin's lamp, rub it and magically it will appear just like that. No! Let me tell you the way it is working for me. As I said, these are my own personal experiences. With deep breathing, knowledge of a strong will, and patience patience-patience, and more patience, my life has changed in such a way that I am happier and healthier and have more and more knowledge. It seems to just come to me now.

When I let go "of faith and hope", I replace them with the will of knowing, which is a knowing of my God's will within me, and knowing how to use this power of God in my life every day. The best and only way I can explain this to you is I am riding in this car and the driver is God. All I have to do is know God's will is in my vein, and I put my best foot forward.

It's a knowing that tomorrow will come and I will be here, knowing where I am going and how I am going to arrive. Knowing that this power is in everyone! Have you ever had a day when everything was just falling into place, one of the best days of your life because you were using this power that God gave to you?

It's not about money. If money makes you happy and money is all you want, then you miss the whole thought! What you will get is peace, love, and happiness. This will also give you the best of health that you could ever have. If you have a long great life, everything else will follow, even money, because you will learn how to attain money.

Understand this, money is just a tool, like everything else, but how you use money determines the outcome of your life.

Most people have the belief that free will means having the right to choose between good or evil, right or wrong, but this is false. These are choices and will is the power of God. I am not a religious person, because religion is manmade. I am a spiritual being created by God who operates on many levels, and one is by energy!

We are all spiritual vessels of this creation and in this physical world, the energy that flows through us and all around us is this energy at our will, given to us by God. I ask no one to believe me, but I know this is who I am and knowing this will work for me because I am getting better every day. Once again, you must have patience. You must also eat the right foods! The right food gives you the right energy for your body to inherit this energy and the right amount of sleep.

You also must understand that negative people are toxic people, people that never have anything good to say about anyone or anything. They always have drama-drama, no matter when you see them; they always have bad news. These are the people that will keep you from finding your true self! You must make a choice, them or _____!! You fill in the blank!

Once you make this connection with the God energy, you can never go back to your old self because your new self is just starting.

It is my purpose to pass this knowledge on and not let it die with me, because one of the richest grounds in the world is the cemetery. So many people went to their graves with information that should have been shared with the world or someone or passed on! Our spouses are living, loving creatures who are emotional at times, and feel pain as we do.

They also have dreams and desires. They are not just someone here to service you for your every want or desire. No!! Sharing is the giving of one's self.

You must celebrate everyday that you have. Out of the untold billions among billions of people that have left this world, and those of us who are here now, must make you realize something is very unique about you.

There's no other person like you. Yes, I speak of God many-many times, and if your eyes and mind are open, I don't have to explain why I do. But let's get back to your uniqueness. Even before this world began, you were already designed in God's thought.

Through your two parents you are here. So why waste all that came together by love's creation. You don't have any right to waste it. You are not to allow someone else to do so either. We all have a great responsibility to ourselves and to the world, and priceless obligation to God for our creations.

CHAPTER NINE: MEN! MEN! MEN!

Come hear ye! How can I as a man learn about my wife, woman, girlfriend, or just a woman friend. Well, one of the best kept secrets is shopping-shopping-shopping! When she's going on her shopping travels, don't stay home watching other men on television, or working on your car, or in your yard.

Go along with her, not just being her driver, bodyguard, or nagger, because she is taking so long. Get into the shopping bug along with her. Watch her, learn her habits, and learn all of her secrets. What are her colors, sizes, and patterns, what makes her eyes light up? Become her shopping partner, and please don't start crying when it's time to pay, or stand as far from the checkout as possible without paying for her Items. Step up and pay for her selections and carry all of her bags!

This message is a very strong connection you are making with your wife and any other woman at that time. Understand women love to show other women that their man loves them by paying for their shopping; believe me, they are almost gleaming with pride! My favorite store is the grocery store; I am like a kid.

Always remember, the food that comes into your house, where did it come from and how does it get in your house? Men, any questions? How many times have you gone to do grocery shopping? So when it's time to pay for the food, don't walk off, ("do-do heads") males.

Today, we as people have lost some of our true and real meaning of life for each other and the world, where our animals live also. We have lost the skills of hard work, truth, trust, respect, love for people, morals, values, and how to be independent to stand alone when all others run away.

Fighting against our own basic good instinct intercedes when we witness wrong in the world and do nothing. This is the loss of integrity by not willing to make sacrifices to make things right in the world. Our kids today have no knowledge of these values or how to practice them, so that they can pass them on to their family. So in turn that their family will be better equipped for today's or tomorrow's world.

CHAPTER TEN: JUST BECAUSE

For those of you who are not familiar with "just because", (fyi) I don't need a calendar or a special day to buy or do something for or with my wife. For the last twenty years, I have bought four dozen roses at 70cm, long stems, and arranged them for her myself, just because! We take trips just because. I love cooking anytime for my wife and myself, just because. Whenever I see something that glitters or is gold, it speaks to me by saying, "I would look nice on your wife".

I will buy them, just because she deserves all this and then more. I love diamonds myself; especially when I wrap them up in a very big box, and putting a couple of bricks inside of the box, so as to give the box some weight, so she can't guess what is inside. I place the diamonds inside so when she opens the box, and to her surprise, the two bricks fall out. The look on her face then is priceless! She then pulls out a perfectly wrapped gift package that holds her true gift! When she opens it and see's her reflection in the diamonds, her smile is all I need from this point on.

Once we were on the west coast at the Wynn hotel, and there was a Cartier shop inside. In the front window was and I did say was, the most beautiful diamond necklace I have ever seen! It started talking to me in that familiar way, and she has that necklace today! Just because!!

First, you must have some Idea of who you are, where you are going, how you are going to get there, and by what means. When you have answers to these questions, and if you are gifted with someone special just for you, then you must have an understanding of how to keep what you want. The woman in my life is without any questions or doubts about her love for me, she loves me for me, and not what I can buy her or do to her, but just for me!

Knowing come hell or high water, she will be there for me and I will always be there for her. There is no one that could trick me, tempt me, or con me, so that I would risk losing my wife and the life we have together. So all you ladies please don't waste my time because there is nothing you have or could give me. I have everything I need!

For all of you that are looking for someone special in your life, maybe you need to find new fishing holes! If your old fishing hole is giving you nothing but throw backs, or half of a person of what you need, ask yourself the question, "what am I doing wrong, and what do I need to do to change? It's a damn shame to live in this beautiful wide world, to never see how other people live, to never travel to see so many wonders and have other people help you expand your new horizons, to find new fishing holes so you can show the world what "you" have to offer.

CHAPTER ELEVEN: FOURTH "S" - SEX

One of the most Important parts of your relationship with your spouse is love making! It's the essence of two people becoming as one in body, spirit, and soul. With your spouse, lovemaking must be as an (art); the touching, giving, and receiving the sexual arousal of each other. I am not going to reveal all of our private lovemaking, but I will talk about what I feel and have learned through my many years of trials and errors of knowledge!

First, there are many ways of having sex! For example, screwing for many personal reasons, we don't need to say the (f) word, and there's the addiction side. Everyone's sexual appetite is very different than yours! But for me, when it comes to my wife, and (only) her, I enjoy the art of making love with and to her. There are so many stages that we have with each other that there are not enough pages or words to explain or express our lovemaking.

Sadly to say, I can't speak for every man from his point of view, but from hearing from so many women speak of their disappointment in lovemaking areas, of their relationships, their marriages, or just by talking to me when I was in the nightclub business for twenty years, believe me, I have heard and seen it all!!

What I found is that most women complain about the lack of emotional connection that is missing from their lovers! In most cases, the sex is great in the beginning, but as time grows within their relationship, their sexual needs grow, but their male companion does not grow along with them, but leaves a void in the women's bedrooms.

I find that most men feel as long as they have an erection and can follow through with intercourse, they have done their part of making love or having sex for the moment. Well guys, this is not true, and you are not bringing all of yourself to your spouse's or lover's needs. Only by me becoming very, very Ill did I accidently find out a lot about myself and my body; the many wonders that laid beneath the surface of my true being!

Let me start by explaining the healing ability that was within my own powers. Yes, I said powers! I learned by different breathing techniques that I can make the palms of my hands heat up and my finger tips to tingle!

I also learned how to transcend my meditation to many higher levels of ability. Now I can will this state of mind at anytime I need to.

CHAPTER TWELVE: TOUCHING

My touching my wife is one of the most important parts of lovemaking to her. First, after a long warm bath, she lay on her stomach and I straddle my wife at her buttocks, play low music, light scented candles.

Now I start from her butt up her lower back, following along her upper back, to the base of her neck, around both sides of her neck, to the back of her ears, then back down unto her shoulder blades, out to both arms, and back to my starting point.

Then I repeat the rubbing all over her back and repeat the rubbing from head to toes; this form of touching makes the lovemaking better, because men, hear me well: when you put your hands on your woman and start head to toe rubbing, feeling her soft essential body, feeling every curve, every emotion inside of her, all of her love enters your body through your hands, your bodies then heat up, and when you start making love to her, you will have the greatest gift the two of you can share with each other.

My own opinion is the greatest creation God gave to this world is "woman". Because of women, I am a man. If for any reason I should wake up and my wife or all women were gone from this world, then it will be my time to check out, because I can't live in this world without women! "Hell no!!" Oh lord, take me with the women. All of my joy and the only joy of living is seeing, hearing, smelling, and knowing that one of God's greatest precious gifts to this world is a woman. Any man that would raise his hand up against a woman, or even his voice, is wrong. I have been guilty of raising my voice, but never again. But to raise his hand is not a strong man, but a coward of a man, and he needs his hands chopped off! When a man raises his hand against a woman he raised his hand against God.

When I look in some women's eyes, I am looking for the twinkle that glows there, meaning whether she is not being loved by a man or enough from her spouse. Men, when you look into your woman's eyes, and there's no twinkle, no glow, no sparks, you are in trouble, deep trouble. When you know you have the right person in your life, they will always express a deep love for you.

They will show respect, and a willing of support in a way only you can understand. This support is when the two of you can read each other's thoughts before words can be spoken. The smile that fills your heart and their eyes touch your soul in ways only they can give to you.

When God created this world and placed man and woman here, he also made sure that no one should be alone in his world. So in his wisdom and grace "God is also a chemist". By using chemistry between a man and woman, one-third of the human population is attracted to each other by his grace and love for us. Just think, there are 6.5 billion people in this world as we speak and one-third of this number were made just for you.

Now, the next three questions to you are, why am I unhappy with the person or persons in my life, why am I all alone, or why can't I find love? Well, only you have this answer for you.

My question to you is, when you see that special someone, do you get this tingle even though it is the next day and are they still on your mind? When you see them again, this feeling is still there. When they see you, they smile and you smile. Both of you are feeling this magic! What the "hell" are you waiting for? But make sure both of you are single!

Being loved by this special person is magical. The love I have for my wife is so strong that I would give my life in order to keep her living on, or to protect her. Not only do I love my wife, but I am "in" love with our relationship.

This is one main reason why I keep in shape and carry a can of whip ass in my back pocket, just in case. Everyone needs someone to love and to be loved in return. There are places on your woman's body that need attention. Just by touching when the two of you are just standing, hold her close and always tell her how much she means to you. Show her the strength of your love for her.

When the two of you are out walking hold her hand even when you have worked a long day. When you get home and see her, your love kicks in and she becomes your main focus, helping her with her needs for you. Only she will let you know of them, but you should already be aware of them all.

When you are touching her, touch the back of her legs behind the knee, kissing these soft areas, rubbing her feet, by taking one of her feet with both of your hands, with two thumbs, slowly rubbing the center of her foot. Then go to the other foot after this, allow her to place her feet on your chest. This is a closely guarded secret of women: they have to put their feet on men's bodies. Then start to touch her thigh with just your finger; a slow light waving rub from her butt to her knees, while whispering love talk to her, asking her how was her day.

Here's one of my best kept lovemaking secrets. While making love to your wife, at the very moment of orgasm, hold her head in your hands and the both of you look directly into each other's eyes while the two of you reach a climax.

The two of you will see each other's soul. I can't explain this experience to you in words that do it justice, but it's a life changing moment for both of you! From my wife I have learned so much about life, love, her, myself, and more than anything else, I have grown more into my own manhood!

Learn how to kiss and caress her body with your lips, hands, and arms. Soft, warm, tingling kisses on her neck, lips, feet, back of her legs, and go as far as you need to go with her. When making love to her, please, please, please express yourself with all of the sounds that you are holding back all of these years, because in your mind a man shouldn't make sounds while making love to his woman. A "real" man just doesn't make sounds, right?! These sounds of lovemaking tell her how much the two of you are loving each other at that exact moment.

Here's a test men!

When your wife, girlfriend, woman-friend is not at home with you and you have the whole day unto yourself, and when you are driving down the street, look over at the seat where she always rides with you. Now, they are no longer sitting there because they are no longer in your life. Men! When you are eating at home, look over at the place where once they usually sat, but they are no longer eating at your table with you, because of your foolish and selfish ways. They are no longer part of your life. Next, when it's time to go to bed, look at the side of the bed that for so many years she slept on, and now it is no longer occupied because of you! Now look at how this picture might look for you, and this is just a test. What would your life be like without them? If you don't feel sadness, loneliness, pain or missing your love one, even if only through this test, you have your answer about your life with or without your spouse or loved one.

For me, this test makes my heart become heavy, sad, and also very painful. Along with this test, it helps keep one grounded about what you have in your life and never to put at risk losing them. It's all in your hands my friends.

I am not perfect, nor am I telling anyone how to live their lives . All I am trying to say is what I have learned that works for me. Use my example as a life learning lesson. A man or woman does not need to do wrong in their lives.

All we have to do is turn on the television or radio, read the newspapers, or look at the internet websites to see so many other peoples relationships falling apart. It's mainly because of their selfishness, mean spirits, cheating assholes, and where did it get them? Nowhere, but it created a great loss. It is the loss of your own humanity, the humiliation of your spouse to their family, friends, and co-workers, and the embarrassment of your love ones, because of your selfish act.

Men please, I plead with you, groom yourself every day and night. Grooming is very important for yourself, and especially in your relationship. Taking a bath or shower is not enough! You must give yourself more time for your grooming. First, your feet are very important. By you walking, standing on your feet from day to day, dead skin builds up on them, thus the expression of alligator feet! This is not just for women; we must get away from this mystical no-no! This is not what a man would do! While you are sitting in the tub, scrub your feet to rid them of dead skin build up. Once you dry off, please, please, please use a body lotion so that your skin can stay moist. Also, use cologne so your woman will tell you how great you smell, how soft and smooth your skin feels, next to hers.

We as men must take better care of our body, go to the doctor by having your yearly checkups, your eye doctor, and dentist. We must stay healthy for ourselves as well as our loved ones. One secret I found out just for myself, is colon cleansing is very-very Important for your health. Very simply to do yourself also!

Also, it's ok to feel sexy men! Women are not the only sexy beings in the world. Don't let them have all the fun by themselves. We too can be sexy and feel good about ourselves. All we have to do is take better care of ourselves.

Before I met my wife, during my nightclub years I was a mixologist. That's a bartender who goes to school to learn how to prepare drinks. During my twenty years stay in the business, I did party, party five nights a week. Drugs, drugs, and more drugs were available. My choice of drink was Louis XII, which is about $2000 a fifth or $200 a shot.

I always had a double if "you" were buying! My choice of drug was cocaine and it was around uncut 80-90 percent purity. I have partied with so many politicians, "stars", sport jocks and every type of person from every walk of life.

Sooner or later, they all will find their way to the nightclub scene. By nature, I am a predominant predator. That means I am very high up the food chain. Anything I want, I got it, anyone I wanted, I had them. Along with little sleep, lots of drinking, so many drugs, bad choice of foods, many years of abusing my body, it all caught up with me in the form of almost renal failure.

I was eating three to four t-bone steaks every day, drinking two six packs of cokes, and constantly eating chocolate candy. I also had a very bad case of bleeding hemorrhoids as well as bad migraines. Before my wife came into my life, doctor's visits were never on my to-do list. After my wife came into my life, with her insistence for me to go to the doctor, on my very first visit my diagnosis was possible renal failure, and a horrible case of hemorrhoids.

Lord only knows what else was going wrong with my health from so many years of self abuse. Now facing kidney failure, my life was about to change and I was even facing death! It was God that saved me from "me", by bringing my wife into my life, to turn my life around.

You see, I was tore up when my wife came along. After two years of treatments and two visits to the hospital involving two surgeries and ultrasound to break up my kidney stones, man, I remember using the restroom trying to urinate. It was very hard then while I was relieving myself for pain came from my head to my toes, because kidney stones the size of marbles were just rolling out of me. I then went into a state of shock due to so much pain.

Next is my trip to the hospital for my hemorrhoid operation. After the operation, I was having to wear adult diapers. All of this was brought on by my not taking care of myself. There were so many other health problems that I was dealing with that it would take up another book. But now, by the grace of God and my loving wife, I was pulled back from the grave. Today, after 15 years of fighting for my life, I am healthier than ever. My kidneys today are in very good shape, no butt problems, and I can stand or sit down without pain.

Today, I am on no medication, plus I visit my personal doctor every year, and if I need to, doctor here I come! Today, I eat the right foods for me. No, I don't use drugs, nor do I drink Louis xiii, or any of his cousins! But after all of my health problems, I have developed a keen sense of smell. For example ,if someone is around me and they have an Illness, when they exhale I can smell their Illness. I can tell you what is wrong with them especially if they have cancer, because cancer smells like very red hot peppers.

One day I got on an elevator and there were people already on it. Once I entered through the door and it closed, I noticed a strange smell, peppers! A week later, I was on another elevator alone, when at a particular stop, a couple entered, and immediately at the moment the doors closed, there came that same smell again!

Right away I overheard the woman talking to the man about his cancer problems. Then came another day when I was riding on an escalator behind some people when I noticed this smell again, and to my surprise, their conversation was about one of them having cancer!

Now, I started noticing when I am around people and they exhale, that if they have a certain Illness from their carbon dioxide I can detect a certain smell of their Illness. Cancer smells to me like a very red hot pepper and the smell is so strong that it takes my breath away! This is a very strange ability because I know private things about people I don't even know! Even if I just see people, I can read them in certain ways; I can know whether they are evil or good even before they open their mouth. I can know before they do if they would lie or not. So for many years I have become aware of my developed abilities. I live everyday to the fullest. So people please, please, let's take better care of ourselves.

I was never a saint. I have been a lost soul in my past! But I will say I have never gone out to hurt or harm anyone. In my mind, I was enjoying the fruits of my labor. I will also say I also have learned one very important thing to do. Learn to forgive yourself first and never dwell on your past, but instead use your past as a learning curve for your future.

"HYPOTHETICAL QUESTION"

People are always crying and complaining about ('Mondays'). We have even given it a name - "blue Monday"! Most people can't wait until Friday and it's just Monday. What about Tuesday, Wednesday, and Thursday? I guess these days don't matter. What if we go to the cemetery and dig up someone out from their resting grave, and take a microphone with us to just ask those that are buried there what would they do or give just to live for one more Monday again, just one? The most precious gift we have here is the time we are given in this world. Take away this time, then what would we have? Love everyday of life, please! Learn how to relax into your soul, and allow your soul to be in control just for a quiet moment every day.

Allow yourself to enjoy your soul. It's been waiting on you. You will notice your timing in everything you do and say becomes perfect timing. Your body will let you know what to eat, what not to eat. You will start looking at life with more enjoyment.

CHAPTER THIRTEEN: FIFTH "S" - SAFE

I am a logical, methodical person! The purpose of most of my subjects is to explain how and why I have reached this point and time in my life, along with my experiences, hoping I may help someone. The responsibility for my wife's safety is at the top of the list of my promises to her. My obligation for her safety is especially from my own vices. On one hand, I am the nicest person anyone can meet or get to know, but by a flip of a switch, I can become the most dangerous person you "don't" want to meet.

My wife calls this second personality a rattlesnake. By making sure I keep my dark side in check, you can believe me, this person scares me sometimes. When I am out in the world, I don't bring anything or anyone back home with me that may cause my wife harm, hurt, or shame!

I make sure that our home is just that, our home. Should something happen to me, her safety is keeping our home in the lifestyle in which she has become accustomed to. I want to make sure that money will never be a problem for her! I make sure that if I break protocol, I will let her know why, when, and my whereabouts, so that she won't worry about me without cause!

No matter where we go or who we are talking to, I don't even care if they don't like us, I demand respect for both of us. Whenever we are out in public, her safety is first for me; as I have said before, I pray that this would never happen, but even if it means giving my life for her without any question, I will! Just for our protection, I will without second guessing my actions, close someone's eyes for good, because I'd rather be judged by twelve than be carried by six!

Her safety is helping her keep her peace of mind, knowing I will stand by her without question. Watching over her and helping her grow by totally supporting her in her adventures while we are on this journey protecting the two of us.

Protecting my wife means on all levels so that even when we are apart, she feels the protection of my strength around her. I am making sure that there are many other principles set in place, so just in case I am not here or there, she has other places and people to call or go to.

We also have in place certain secret code words, so if and when we use then, we both know of danger, or it's time to leave immediately wherever we are.

"Hypothetical"!!!!! To Men"" What if!!!!? Let's Say Suppose?

How do you describe safety for your spouse/or woman?

1. How safe is your spouse when you are cheating on your wife/woman, having sex outside your marriage/relationship, bringing back to them a deadly std_____?

2. Now let's ask all of your other women how do they feel about contracting this deadly std from you_____?

3. Let's say you get another woman pregnant, but for the time being, your wife has no Idea about your new baby on the way. What would be your next move_____?

How would your wife handle this news? You can't answer this for her so don't even try.

How safe would she feel when your other woman finds a way to tell your wife about the two of you having a baby_____?

After working a long week, now it's the weekend and Friday night, with the night fever in your blood, you get to hit the streets, but as you always do, you go out without your wife. You're gone all night, even some of you ("do-do" heads) are gone all weekend, then show up back home Monday evening after work, as though everything is just fine!

Now, while you were not at home, your family or your wife faced so many dangers alone; home invasion, rape, murder, house on fire, sudden Illness, maybe rushed to the hospital, but they were just worried about you and if you're ok!!

How safe can your family/or wife be_____? Your answer is_____?

Let's talk about your "boys", your homey's, always dropping in, not even calling first. You can bet your ass ("do-do" head) that at least two of your "boys" would have your wife in a New York minute, even rape her, because you trust your "boys" over your wife's safety.

I don't want to sound as if I am preaching to anyone, or coming down on anyone, but from being a very mature and knowledgeable man, I know there are so many women left home alone. Reason being, their men still don't nor want to understand how important their presence at home means to their family/or wife; for you to be with her at night is so Important because outside forces also know when the man of the house is not at home at night. You see because they also are not at home. When they see you out partying (or as today's women call men whores) and you are whoring around, there is nothing to stop them from going over to "your" home, knowing that your wife/family is there without you_____!!!!

We as men must understand the more people you have over your home, the more danger it is for your family or even yourself; even having people working outside around your house, in your yard. These people could be predators, running their mouths out in the street to other people about personal information about you and your family and your home.

This alone will endanger your family. Has this even crossed your mind with the world as it is today? Or maybe you have your head stuck in the sand and your ass is open for anyone to stick you in your_____? Safety must be first for your wife.

Even in the Bible and I am not going to tell you where to find this verse, but believe me it's there, reads as follows: the (sons) of God looked down on earth and saw the daughters of man, came down from heaven and lay with them.

My point: If the (sons) of God left heaven when they saw God's greatest art work, women, then woman is the greatest gift from God, given to have as our mate, lover, companion and wife. Why can't we keep them safe and love them truly as they love us?

My knowledge about the story of the (sons) of God from the Bible came from me reading the Bible three different times from the beginning to the end. One point I tell to all don't just take someone else's word, search and find Important information about life for yourself, then research more and more. Because the truth is always running away from you. Reason is as we keep after the truth on our journey, we find out about ourselves, who we really are, and what we really can do for "ourselves" and our family. Most of all it shows us what we can do for the world as a whole!

Understand, in any relationship there will be ups and downs, no matter how much love there is. It's a work in progress. Every day brings new challenges, and it takes the two of you to make this love work. Very Important note: every woman, every man, boy and girl must have their own place in this world, by letting the world know that you are here!!

CHAPTER FOURTEEN: THE SIXTH "S" - SPIRITUAL

After every night, morning comes along with the rising of the sun! Even if there's an overcast sky of clouds, the sun always shines. Night once again returns with the greeting of Mr. Moon under a starlit night, gazing up and out into the far distance worlds of the cosmos! In every walk of life, from one corner of the world connecting with the other three, we as humans live in the world together but still so far apart.

From man comes so many types or kinds of religion with their "God". Their God is better than everyone else's God, which only separates us even more.

The most precious gift we have is not what we have or who we have in our lives, but it's the time we are given here on this planet. This means we are given a great gift from God. With his love and understanding, we can take this wonderful gift and go farther. We are not alone in this world. Look around us from every created life form, as in angels from within the realm of heaven, and most of all, God himself.

Sadly, we are no closer to the real meaning of why are we here, where did we come from, how did we get here, nor are we closer to God, or the real question in all of our minds, does God exist at all and where might we find God?

These are once again my own thoughts, my own opinions, in my lifetime, my experiences, my answers from my questions I am not asking or telling anyone what to do with their lives. How to find your answers just in case, should there be questions from you. All I am doing throughout these pages of my life is that I have found something from a connection I have with God. That my life has turned around in such a wonderful way that it could only be explained by God!

Society dictates to our parents, teachers, preachers, and grandparents that we should all be tried and true for goodness, love thy neighbor, love thy enemy, care for each other, be your brother's keeper, help those that are in need, but what they don't tell us is that most of those that are less fortunate, the same ones that we extend our hearts, homes, and hands will be the very ones that are out to harm, maim, cripple, or even kill us. They use our kindness against us as a weakness for their advantage. We must retrain our minds and hearts that everyone is not our friend.

There are many, many mean people in this world that are out to do us harm. Sadly to say, they will use you up over and over while keeping a smile on their faces, with lies on their tongues. Just as fast as they can, they move on to their next victim.

This is the way they view the world. There is nothing or no one that can or will change these people! Yes, I know about God's power, but these are people whom are just bad asses period. God in his own time and place will deal with them. We must be prepared for them and deal with them before they deal the kiss of death unto us.

Bottom line, it's either them or us! Most religions preach to us about a spiritual devil and his demons. My life lessons tell me to be more aware of these human two legged devils and demons who can reach out and do us all harm and even death!

Family members, spouses, lovers, friends, homeboys, home girls, co-workers, and anyone that this shoe fits, put them in these categories. This is someone that never has anything good to say or offer to anyone, and most times is always complaining about their life, not even saying good morning or have a nice day.

Let's say what if your homeboy or home girl is always bragging on how they are always looking to get over on someone, how bad they have done someone else, thinking how slick they are over other people. They are going to get even against someone. Now let's add all of this up just to see what would we come up with. Without you giving your answer I'll give you one, because all of you are going to keep saying that they are my "family or friends". They are my homeboys/home girls and they wouldn't do that to "me". Well! Then your head is stuck in the sand and your rear end is stuck up in the air for these same people to "f" you again and again! These people understand only one thing or rather three things; me, myself, and I! If you or let's say we, know of someone that is evil to others or is doing wrong, we still call them our friend and turn our heads away from their evil deeds. Then we are just as guilty and wrong as they are, but deep down inside of us, we already know this, don't we?

Telltale signs are right in our faces, for example your loved one or spouse doesn't help you around the house. You are always cleaning up behind them and they never offer any help to you. You always have to ask and ask, and more asking for money to help you around the house, toward paying bills, so they can have something as simple as toilet paper, so that they can wipe their butt. Then they are telling you how they truly feel about you right now, by ignoring you.

These are the telltale signs right in your face. Now from this point, what are we to do? It's all up to you! We are created spiritual beings, created in the Image of God, by God, for his purpose! Why do we allow or let ourselves fall for other people's demands? Really, I must say these are tricks and we are not following our own minds. By allowing so many outside influences to affect us, into their darkness when we are children of light, we can only blame ourselves.

Here's another story from the bible. I don't say bible verses about Jesus speaking to a group of people. Jesus' words to those people were as follows: "I say unto thee, ye are (gods)", small 'g'. Now, how you interpret these words are left up to us, not someone else's version of Jesus' words. In other words, mainly these people are not Jesus and to believe and trust your own minds. They will turn these words around to mislead us from our true nature. Please trust your own mind. Jesus is opening our minds. We have the ability to do anything or become anyone we want to be.

The same energy that was there with God when he created all of life and all therein is the same energy that burns in every star in the cosmos, and it is the same energy within us, just in human form. We must reconnect our energy back to our creator, becoming once again spiritual beings of light. I know your question is what do all of these other subjects have to do with (which) "S" of love for my wife? Well, I hope these other subjects will awaken your spiritual being to the point of awareness of what it will take.

First, know how to use one of my "s" of loving your wife, from a spiritual realm, because then it should come natural from you, in which only you can continue to give to her. God's energy: electromagnetism and electricity is God's energy source in our bodies, in all living animals, trees, flowers and every creation. Objects flow with this energy from the beginning of the creation of all life forms; this energy was with God in the beginning and still is with God. Our planet earth is a living being of a higher form, which also sustains us with this energy. Have you ever been touched by someone and received an electric shock, or you touched something or someone and then received a shock? The sun, which is 93 million miles away, is big enough that you could put 1300 planets the size of our planet inside of it. This same energy is in the sun that gives life to us all.

Now imagine what kind of power it took to make the sun, a big ball of fire that has been burning at a guess of about five billion years. We can't even imagine this amount of time in any life form. Yes, life form is what the sun is also. No one could have made this ball of fire with their bare hands!

God, who also created us, and I can say that made us, since we are his creation, also created the sun, plus trillions on top of trillions of other stars that are bigger than our own sun. So many others are bigger than our sun compared to even more in the cosmos, which can make our sun as small as a pinhead. This is mind boggling!!!

Light travels at 186,000 miles per second. It will take light 100,000 light years to travel from one end of our Milky Way system to the other side. Light travels 5.9 trillion miles in "one" light year. Our Milky Way galaxy is just one out of a billion-trillion other galaxies in which we could not even imagine in our wildest imagination how many there truly are.

Yes, again the energy that was with God when he created us was created in all of the galaxies, meaning the known universe as well as the unknown universes. All we have to do is to love each other, reconnecting this energy with God's energy, rising above and beyond our earthly emotions, by his will becoming knowledgeable of our own will. Now let me say again, I am not trying or asking anyone to change their minds, thoughts, or hearts. These are all my own personal experiences.

It's my personal feeling and duty to reveal this information to the world, knowing that this will open hearts and minds to your spiritual being. We all must find our true selves, in order to know what really works for each one of us, because what works for me might not work for you.

This is your journey as it's my journey. I have found my right path, so please find yours! When I reconnected to the energy of God, I became this spiritual being, knowing the power of God's will on a spiritual level, has opened my eyes, body, mind, and soul, unto unlimited sources of energy that never stops flowing from God! But first, understand one Important thing; you must clear your mind and heart of evil, clear your mind of all doubts, never speaking evil about anyone, or things, being very selective about what comes out of your mouth, because you will be able as so many smart people know and say, "If you can imagine it you can achieve it!"

We must never again tell (lies), never. When you understand the power we all have to (will) this energy from God, you must stay pure at heart to yourself. If you even try to go back to your old self, this energy is going to let you know right then and there that you are back in darkness again!

I mean instantly! You will hurry back to the right track, because your old track will scare the living "hell" out of you. So if you are sincere and happy as you are now, then stay as you are. But for me, I am very fortunate to have this knowledge of the power of energy and willpower. Yes, I also still get sick, bleed when I cut my fingers, yell when I hit my knee, feel pain; I am still human and have life as everyone else. The only difference for me is I have a better knowledge about this energy of God that he gave to the world, so that we can will this energy as we want it to be, as our connection we have with God.

I have an understanding of how to make my life better and more bearable, as well as how to be in more control of my day! We are vessels that God passed on his knowledge to, information through his will in all of us, so that we can live as the creation in which he created us to be! I don't want to go to my grave without telling the world of this wonderful gift we all share together. Can we just imagine where the world would be if we all worked together as one people, one race, the human race? All I can see is heaven here on earth for us all!!

This energy is the gift that God gave to the world. It's an unlimited source of power just for us. This energy comes in many forms. It comes in ways that words can't explain. All of us have had thoughts of someone in our minds, and as soon as those thoughts are gone, in a short moment, that person will appear from nowhere. We all then say I was just thinking about you/them; and they just walked up (o' man).

Now any questions I have when these or any questions are in my mind about anything or anyone, then all the answers for the questions come in clearly and soundly.

Example: here's a way this energy works for me. I am driving down the highway just like any city driving. I drove up on all lanes blocked and everyone had stopped, for many various reasons; so in my mind in a very calm way, I asked and commanded a way for me to keep moving. Just as fast as these thoughts passed through my mind, a lane magically opened up for me and I started moving on my way.

There are so many examples of my experiences that I started learning more about how this energy works, and not using it in any other way but for positive acts. I could talk about more experiences but they would fill up a library of books.

I was having trouble with my lawn mower one day after I let my neighbor use it. My mower started to run badly and kept cutting off. I had no idea what was wrong. A couple of weeks went by and while I was shopping in Home Depot one day, a man just walked up and asked me about spark plugs, out of the blue. His question was that he needed to find the right spark plug for "his" lawn mower. After about five minutes we found the right plug he needed so he thanked me and started walking away. Just at that exact moment, I turned in the direction in which the man had starting walking away, and it couldn't have been more than a 1/2 second, and he was nowhere to be found. We all know how long and how high the aisles are in Home Depot, so even if this man was a world class runner, there was no way he could have left so quickly from that aisle. Before I could see him again, before my mind could wonder about this person, my mind kept repeating - "spark plug, you may need a plug for 'your' mower". So I bought a new spark plug, took out the old one and replaced it with the new one, and just like a brand new mower, it cranked right up and has been running without any problems. I haven't had any more trouble! I have been in Home Depot many times and never has anyone stopped and asked me for any advice. Once again, this energy also comes in human form with the answers you need.

I have been told by many medical professionals that passing a kidney stone is like a woman giving birth to a baby. Well, as I stated before, I was at a point of kidney failure. I recall one particular moment when I was at work early one morning when without warning, I dropped to my knees so fast with pain, because I was having a kidney stone trying to pass. I lay on the floor about an hour in deep pain. I finally got myself up and drove myself home, so that I could hopefully rest. When I arrived home, to my surprise, my wife had just walked in about five minutes before I got there.

She immediately drove me to the hospital. After we arrived there and after giving all pertinent information at the registration desk, we then went through ('those doors')! If anyone has been to the emergency room, then all of you know about 'those doors'. A nurse started asking me questions about my condition and all I could say was a moan and groan, "ooh-ooh-ooh!" She then gave me something for pain and after twenty minutes or so, my pain was gone. Right then the nurse came back in the room and asked me how was I doing and how bad was my pain. Before I could get a word out, my wife and the nurse started laughing at the same time. The nurse replied to me, " oh so you can talk after all!"

Here's another moment of all the right people being in the right places at the right time for me. Here is this energy working for me and it can for you too!

(A day in time)

Here's a day that changed my whole life, in an instant. Just two words can change your life! One day I was using a table saw, cutting a cabinet door down one side. On this particular cutting, I wore gloves and as I fed the wood through the saw, the blade grabbed the thumb part of my glove on my left hand, "cutting the thumb completely off!!!" At this point I then turned the saw off! The whole room became instantly quiet, no sound, no movement, and it was as if time itself stopped. As I stood there looking at my glove, looking at where the thumb part of the glove "used" to be, it was no longer there!! I slowly pulled the glove off my hand, and as the glove pulled away from my hand exposing what was underneath, my thumb was "gone"! Cut off at the joint!! All that was left was a short bloody stub! I was in disbelief of what had just happened to me; shock would be a better word!

Instead of losing my mind, I kept my head on straight. At that very moment, as if my mind itself took over, and a voice from my mind said, "let's move it, let's move it, there's no time to lose, snap to it, look behind you on the floor to your right, you will see your thumb! Now pick it up, we need to put it on Ice, and as quickly as we can get over to the hospital to get help!!!""

Fortunately for me again, a friend was close by. I called out to him in a very calm voice that I needed him to take me to the hospital, because I had cut my thumb off!! At that moment, he started to laugh because he thought I was playing a joke on him, until I showed him my thumb in a bag of Ice!! His laughter turned into terror on his face and in his voice. Finally, we were on our way to the hospital, and while in the car he said to me, how can I be so calm and relaxed? All I could relay to him at that time was I really don't know! Once we arrived at the emergency room front desk, I had to explain what was my reason for being there. So in my calm voice, I replied that I had cut my thumb off!! Again, there was that shocked look on people faces, terror in their voices as if it was 'their' thumb cut off instead of 'mine'.

There was a lady behind me listening to my story who immediately went and got a wheelchair for me, and had me to sit down in it. It's so amazing that when someone is in need of help, total strangers will give of themselves to comfort and give us all help.

Again, here's this energy of God stepping in to see us all through. Then my wheelchair person asked me if I was in pain, and for the first time at that very moment through it all pain showed up and showed out! Pain as though my arm was on fire!! What was so amazing at this point of my crisis was at no time was I in pain, nor was there a lot of blood before I was asked the question. I can remember a little bleeding on the ground next to my car before we went off to the hospital.

I now am back behind those double doors again and a doctor was there in the room before I was, a first I believe. I was given something for the pain by him. The doctor looked at my hand, then at my thumb in the bag of Ice, and he then replied "you may have saved your thumb by putting it in ice, because it still had color, meaning blood was still inside of it". He then referred me over to a hand surgical specialist at another hospital across town. My next ride in the ambulance was off to the hand specialist. Upon arrival at the hospital, the staff started preparing me for surgery, which lasted for seven hours, followed by four days in the hospital, and eight months of rehabilitation. My thumb was saved and even the fingernail has grown back!

Now you can't tell which thumb was cut off unless you look very closely. Again, all of the right people were in place at my time of need.

I don't believe in coincidence. My reason for these stories of my life is to let you realize this energy and once you understand the power of this energy, how it works in it's many forms, this ability we were given by God, free will therefore means the ability to will this energy to work for us all! I am not a saint, nor am I perfect. I tried perfect. It was boring and turned all of my friends and love ones against me. I am just a human being from God, giving my life's gifts. I have come to a knowing and knowledge of understanding the wisdom within. I found out about this life giving energy force that is all around us. It's in all of our foods, all of our waters, all of our plants, and mother earth produces this life force for us as long as we are pure in heart and from a spiritual knowledge, we can make our lives better. But evil doers, negative people, hateful people, block this energy so therefore it won't work for them.

Everything they do from their emotions won't work right for them. They are unsure why things always go wrong for them, and they are never getting ahead in life. What they don't understand is first, to know and respect this energy. Secondly, to learn about what is this energy, why this energy is here, and how to use it to work for good in your life. Also, where to find the true knowledge for us to reach to the spiritual realm of the connection we all have within us. All but understand this. For all of the wrong we have done in this world, and before this energy works for you, you must pay for all of your debts of wrongness or evil. Before all of us leave this world, we will pay for all I mean all the wrong we have done. No one will leave this world owing this world, without paying for their evil/wrongness. For all of the righteousness you do, you will learn of this gift from God. This life energy will work in your life, give you wisdom, and help you gain knowledge with a better understanding of life. It will always be with you. Your life will be enriched more than you could ever imagine!

"Remember 23"

Yea though I walk through the valley of the shadow of death I will fear no evil; For thou art with me. Thy rod and thy staff; they comfort me.

Having this knowing with me, along with the knowledge of life energy of mother earth, I know there is no one or nothing I need to fear or any doubt about my ability to reach my true spiritual being. Let's talk about why God is punishing you! We all know some of these people, and some of them are you. "Why is God punishing me, why is my luck so bad, and why can't I get ahead?"

Well first, God is 'not' punishing us! We are punishing ourselves and don't even understand or have the knowledge of why it's our own lack of the God energy that is doing us in. Most people take the easy way out, always blaming someone else for our short comings. Excuses, excuses, rather than accepting the responsibility on our own heads! This energy has laws and guidelines just like every other form of God's works and laws given to us.

So you can continue to run you head into a brick wall blaming everyone or everything as to why we are having such a hard time and asking the same old questions you always ask. Why is God punishing me? I go to church every Sunday, I pay my tithes, I love thy neighbor, I honor thy father and mother, I work hard! What we first don't know is about this energy and how it works for us all. I am not asking anyone to believe me about this form of this gift from God to us, no!

But all I can do is to tell you about this wonderful gift that I have come to know of, to understand it, how this energy works, where it came from, why it's here for us all, how great and wonderful it is; how it has changed and made my life better, along with the healing powers, making my life more plentiful, not just material matters, but with the right people in my life.

I hear so many people giving others advice about where to go to find that right someone, but they are falling so short with that advice, because it's not the wrong places that people go to find that right person, but what they are doing is finding the wrong people to look at!

Let's just say you started cooking, and 10 minutes into your cooking you forgot that you needed something else from the store. So now we are at the store and you left the stove on to continue cooking because you were just going to be 5 minutes out and back. But, we ran into a long lost friend, got to talking, and time just flew by. We just forgot about our cooking and there's no one at home to turn off the stove. So about 1 & 1/2 hours later, we finally headed back home.

As soon as you turned into your street, I don't have to tell you what happened, do I, but let me tell you anyway! There are fire trucks and neighbors where your house once was, because you left your stove on! We, yes I said we, burned down our home and now we have no home! The next thing to come out of your mouth is, "Why is God punishing me? What did I do to deserve this? God was not the one that left the stove on, and then went to the store staying 1 & 1/2 hours did he? We are always putting blame on others but not ourselves; if you would just have taken the time to turn off the stove. Always make sure your home is secure before you leave, because believe it or not, something always comes up when you least think it will. So, if you need more time away from your home, your baby, your whatever, make sure it is safe there for you and them. Make sure they will be there for you to come back to and just take the time to do so, please.

CHAPTER FIFTEEN: HELLO
WEEKEND WARRIORS

We are all guilty of being weekend warriors. When Monday comes all we hear is blue Monday, oh how I hate Monday and I can't wait for Friday! But today is just Monday, so what makes Monday so bad? Now, today is Monday and we are already wanting Friday. Well, let's go to the cemetery and ask all that lay there as their final resting place, if they could rise again able to relive Monday-Tuesday-Wednesday-Thursday, what would they give or do if they could live again just on these four days that most of us hate. Monday, dread Tuesday, and Wednesday is looked upon as hump day. Thursday is only the day before Friday. We can't wait for Thursday to be over. Now it's Friday - hello! Everybody comes to life, electricity is in the air, a pep is in everyone's walk, and a smile is on their faces.

Every Monday, all we do is rush time. We can't wait for Friday every week of our lives! Do we understand what we really are doing by rushing time just for the weekend? See, that means Monday, Tuesday, Wednesday, and Thursday mean nothing to us. We must learn to enjoy every moment we have on this planet, every second of life is a gift, precious moments of life, memories with love ones, and how many babies are born on these days. Just imagine how our lives would be without these days. Now here comes Friday, that one day we all are waiting for - 'payday'!

Saturday, party hardy, shopping, shopping, spend, spend and more spending. Sunday, well we all know about Sunday. Now put the brakes on because here comes Mr. Monday again and we start crying all over again. We can't wait for Friday again. We spent all of our little monies over the weekend and that's why we are called weekend warriors. Also, why we can't wait for Friday again and again! It's really not Friday that we are really looking forward to, let's be honest, if Monday was payday, then Monday becomes our Friday!!

CHAPTER SIXTEEN: "LET'S BLAME GOD"

You know you have diabetes, but you won't go and get a checkup with a real doctor. You're eating anything you want to eat, not eating all of the right foods for your condition, (no)! Then, when you lose one kidney or both, a leg, or any limb because all you had to do was get to a doctor or stay with your doctor's orders, you can have a better life.

High blood pressure runs in your family but you're not going to the doctor for a checkup. Years pass you by, then one day at work you pass out! Guess who is here? Mr. High blood pressure. You die on the job from it. Yet, if you went years earlier to the doctor, your family would not be without you.

When you were alive, did you ever think about your family? What would they do if something happened to you? Guess what? It finally happened. Do you remember that day you were in line at the grocery store when you got to the cashier? When she finally cashed you out, she gave you $50 back more than she should have. Knowing she made a mistake, you said nothing, even though this was her very first day on the job. Even if she was your daughter's age, while you were being checked out by her, she told you all about herself, and how happy she was having her first job!

But being your get over self, you kept the money, left the store in a hurry. Now two weeks later on your way to work, you ran over something hard in the road, got two flat tires, and also damaged two rims; having to have your car towed to a shop, lose a whole day out of work, here is what karma brought you after your measly $50. Go back two weeks earlier. Do you remember the get over queen or king? What did that $50 get you?

1) a day out of work

2) 2 new tires

3) 2 new rims

4) tow charges

Karma might not be through with you yet. Karma is very real! I remember I was standing in line at a store to buy a soda, and while in line this total stranger said, "Excuse me sir, did you drop this money on the floor, because it was down by your feet?" He then said the amount, "7 one hundred dollar bills!" That's seven hundred dollars! I said to him, "no sir, that's not my money". At that moment, the man said he was going to turn the money over to the cashier, and that's exactly what he did! We both went our separate ways. Yes, I could have lied and said yes, I dropped the money and it was my money. But I am not a liar because the money was not mine. I also hoped that the person who lost it came back to claim their money.

Once again, you sometime ask yourself, where did this person come from who found the money on the floor, and then, ask the person in front of them in line if they dropped seven hundred dollars on the floor? I am not a saint, nor am I a liar. Once you tell a lie, then you get on a roll and you can't stop! We all are open vessels of God, so there's nothing that goes unnoticed or unheard by him. Remember this! God explains this energy better than I ever could and tries to make it clear to all of us. He gave us his words, and he speaks very clearly about his message regarding everything.

This energy was with him in the beginning when he (willed) it into who we were yesterday, who we are today, and who we will become in the future! In the beginning, God said let there be light. This energy flows throughout the universe and is still going on today all around us. All we have to do is ask for the knowledge along with the wisdom and understanding of the wonderful gift of this energy! So we can truly become the spiritual creator of God's creation.

The other side of this wonderful gift is just the opposite of good, the flip side is evil. We the people, stand by watching our country destroy and kill other people around the world. Our elected politicians lie to us. Knowing they are corrupt, we turn our heads and keep voting them back in office, time after time. This corruption created in our hearts returns to us in many forms; i.e., hurricanes, tornadoes, floods, or bad storms. Until we understand this energy of the planet and how God put it in place to protect, heal, and watch over us, we must pay for all of our wrong, before any of us leaves this world.

We will be made to pay for all of our wrong and no one will be allowed to leave owing this world anything. Just imagine, if we as people of this world work together as one race, the human race, toward making all living better as the creator created us to live, the wonder we could accomplish together! We as human beings must understand the meaning of karma: the totality of one's acts in each state of one's existence. This means what we do good or bad will return back to us all, no matter what or who we believe in. Yes, God will forgive us for all of our wrong, but this energy that we are all connected to will make us pay for our wrong in this world. Just stop and look around us. What we have in this beautiful world we have been given from God. So many of his personal gifts to us; this is his love for us, and all we have to do is God's will.

I am not trying or asking anyone to change their ways or beliefs about how they should live their lives, but I feel it's my duty as a vessel of this information from a higher source to give to whomever is willing to listen, in hopes that this information might help someone to open their minds to live a better life, knowing this knowledge will help make this world the place God created for us all to live in as spiritual beings.

Genesis:

After Adam and Eve broke God's command, most people were taught this was the main reason why they were put out of the garden, but it was just 'part' of this reason. The main reason was as it is written, God said, 'let ("us") banish them from the garden before they eat from the tree of knowledge and become 'Gods' like ("us")!!! The tree of knowledge was this tree he created and why was this tree one of many there in this garden? What was the purpose of this tree?

Mainly understand this! If Adam and Eve ate from this tree of knowledge, they would have become as Gods. Knowledge is a very important key of God's consciousness that we all must acquire in our own lifetime. Now my next question is who are those referred to as ('us')? It was also used when God created man, remember let ('us') make man in ('our') Image. There are those that would say (us and our) mean God the son and the Holy Spirit.

Please don't be bamboozled by other people's opinions along with them telling you that God told them to tell you something, or God spoke to them about you. So whatever they tell you from this point on you must believe whatever they tell you to do? You must follow their every word because God tells them so! Let's step out of our shell and please listen to your own heart. When God needs to speak to you or us, he will speak 'directly' to you, not through someone else! When you hear people saying they are doing God's work, the work they are doing is their own work!

God created everything and everyone without man's help. God's work has already been done, set in his creation, and never needing help from one of his creations. Think please for once in your lives. Start thinking for 'ourselves', and we will find out that we are thinkers and problem solvers on our own, with God's help and energy.

God gives to us all his gifts of mercy. With all that we have been given from God we must understand how unique we all are as individuals of God's creation. In this life, please believe whatever you must, but let's not waste this life we have here. Live up to your true being as the unique and wonderful person you know you are.

"THE PROMISE"

Please know this - God promised that he would never become so angry at man that he would destroy the world again. In keeping his promise, God placed a rainbow in the sky as a reminder of his promise to the world!!

I have come to know many people in this world and when I met my wife, I had no Idea that she came from a great family. For this I will always be thankful to God, for my wonderful family which has come into my life because of her. They all have my utmost respect. When I hear women are looking for a 'good' man, well here are some great 'men and women';

MY FAMILY:

IN MEMORY OF:

MR. CLARENCE "COTTON" CLARK

MRS. CAROLINE "YAMMY" CLARK

DR. CLARENCE "POOKEY" CLARK

DR. JOYCE CLARK

DR . CAROL ANN CLARK-ADAMS

MRS. ERNESTINE "AUNTIE" EMBRY (THE BEST)

OTHER FAMILY MEMBERS:

MR. CARMICHAEL CLARK	MR. CAMERON "RONI' GAMBLE
MRS. SHIRLEY CLARK	MRS. PRINCESS GAMBLE
DR. CLAYTON CLARK	MISS CAMERON 'GRACIE' GAMBLE
DR. THEORIA CLARK	MR. & MRS. COLBERT MASTIN
MRS. COLLEEN CLARK "BOP" ABIDI	MR. & MRS. CULLEN MASTIN
MR. TROY "TROUBLE" WEAVER	CHE-DOG ABIDI

MRS. CAROLYN "BEAUTIFUL" WEAVER

TERRENCE ROBINSON

MR. & MRS. HOPKINS (AKA BIG SISTER VIRGIE)

MITCHIE & CHANGIE

MRS. NELLIE & ENTIRE NEAL FAMILY

MR. & MRS. CLARENCE JULIAN CLARK

MR. CALVIN

CARMEN CLARK

KEVIN CLARK

WAYDAL SANDERSON & FAMILY

COTY & CHARI CLARK

ALLISON & PRISCILLA

TONY WEAVER

SHAUNTE & ONJELIC

SHIBA (GODMOTHER)

CARLISSA

RAYMOND & ANGELA

SPECIAL THANKS TO MR. GARY GUNTER, DAVID TUCK, DON GARRARD AND THE SPECIALTY FINISHES FAMILY: CHRIS LYERIA, SHELIA LYERIA, CHRIS EVANS, BILL CASEY, RUSSELL DILL, CHRISTINE BROWN, STEPHEN MAY, DEWYE CASON, RANDY NELSON, TOM MCLAIN, RICKY RICARDO, MARK KEHELEY (THANKS FOR THE JOKES!) KEN, PAT, GEORGE, SAM, RYAN, JILL, JACK

BACK PAGE OF BOOK!

I have been given so many wonderful gifts from God, such as his love, my loving wife, the gift of knowledge to know of his wisdom, and knowledge of how to will God's energy of this world! There is so much sadness that I see in so many people's eyes, especially in the eyes of so many beautiful women, that I must write these truths! I will never be unfaithful to my wife, so this is the only way I can share part of me with them, in knowing that passing on this information may bring fullness. Making this connection to their true spiritual existence will help them find true happiness and their own strength within this energy!

Inspirational and Motivational Quotable Quotes

We can only learn to love by loving – Iris Murdoch

An eye for eye only ends up making the whole world blind –
Gandhi

The only way of finding the limits of the possible is by going
beyond them into the impossible – Arthur C. Clarke

We are what we repeatedly do. Excellence, therefore,
is not an act but a habit – Aristotle

Work spares us from three evils: boredom, vice, and need –
Voltaire

Fortune favors the brave – Publius Terence

I love you, not only for what you are, but for what I am
when I am with you – Roy Croft

A kiss is a lovely trick, designed by nature, to stop words when
speech becomes superfluous – Ingrid Bergmen

To laugh often and love much...to appreciate beauty,
to find the best in others, to give one's self...this is to have
succeeded – Ralph Waldo Emerson

Let the wife make the husband glad to come home, and let him make her sorry to see him leave – Martin Luther

When you judge another, you do not define them,   you define yourself – Wayne Dyer

To think is easy. To act is hard. But the hardest thing in the world is to act in accordance with your thinking – Goethe

Act as if what you do makes a difference. It does – William James

When wealth is lost, nothing is lost; when health is lost, something is lost; when character is lost, all is lost – Billy Graham

Our greatest glory is not in never failing, but in rising every time
we fall – Confusius

All our dreams can come true, if we have the courage to pursue
them – Walt Disney

Great spirits have always encountered violent opposition from
mediocre minds – Einstein

We are still masters of our fate. We are still captains of our souls
– Winston Churchill

The reasonable man adapts himself to the world;
the unreasonable one persists in trying to adapt the world to
himself.   Therefore all progress depends on the unreasonable man
– George Bernard Shaw

The journey is the reward – Chinese Proverb

People are like stained-glass windows. They sparkle and shine
when the sun is out, but when the darkness sets in,
their true beauty is revealed only if there is a light from within
– Elizabeth Kubler Ross

Within each of us lies the power of our consent to health and
sickness, to riches and poverty, to freedom and to slavery. It is we
who control these, and not another – Richard Bach

To be yourself in a world that is constantly trying to make you something else is the greatest accomplishment
– Ralph Waldo Emerson

The greatest weakness of most humans is their hesitancy to tell others how much they love them while they're alive – Orlando Battista

Only when we give joyfully, without hesitation or thought of gain, can we truly know what love means – Leo Buscaglia

We come to love not by finding a perfect person, but by learning to see an imperfect person perfectly – Sam Keen

Love cures people—both the ones who give it and the ones who receive it – Karl Menninger

The choice that you, as a Soul, have in relation to anything is always to be loving. Do you understand that this is the divine purpose that all of us as humans have been given—to love unconditionally? – John Morton

You will find as you look back upon your life that the moments when you have truly lived are the moments when you have done things in the spirit of love – Henry Drummond

Being deeply loved by someone gives you strength while loving someone deeply give you courage – Lao Tzu

Several Quotes from Oprah Winfrey:

Think like a queen. A queen is not afraid to fail. Failure is another steppingstone to greatness

Turn your wounds into wisdom

Understand that the right to choose your own path is a sacred privilege. Use it. Dwell in possibility

Unless you choose to do great things with it, it makes no difference how much you are rewarded, or how much power you have

What God intended for you goes far beyond anything you can imagine

What I know is, is that if you do work that you love, and the work fulfills you, the rest will come

When someone shows you who they are, believe them the first time

You CAN have it all. You just can't have it all at once

If you want to accomplish the goals of your life, you have to begin with the spirit

It isn't until you come to a spiritual understanding of who you are- not necessarily a religious feeling, but deep down, the spirit within – that you can begin to take control

Lots of people want to ride with you in the limo, but what you want is someone who will take the bus with you when the limo breaks down

Luck is a matter of preparation meeting opportunity

My idea of heaven is a great big baked potato and someone to share it with

My philosophy is that not only are you responsible for your life, but doing the best at this moment puts you in the best place for the next moment

Passion is energy. Feel the power that comes from focusing on what excites you

Real integrity is doing the right thing, knowing that nobody's going to know whether you did it or not

Surround yourself with only people who are going to lift you higher

The biggest adventure you can take is to live the life of your dreams

The greatest discovery of all time is that a person can change his future by merely changing his attitude

The more you praise and celebrate your life, the more there is in life to celebrate

The thing you fear most has no power. Your fear of it is what has the power. Facing the truth really will set you free

The whole point of being alive is to evolve into the complete person you were intended to be

OTHER QUOTABLE QUOTES

A successful marriage requires falling in love many times, always with the same person – Mignon Mclaughlin

All that we love deeply becomes a part of us – Helen Keller

The most important thing in life is to learn how to give out love, and to let it come in – Morrie Schwartz

It is love alone that leads to right action. What brings order in the world is to love and let love do what it will – Jiddu Krishnamurti

Of all forms of caution, caution in love is perhaps the most fatal to true happiness – Bertrand Russell

Love is the condition in which the happiness of another person is essential to your own – Robert Heinlein

Some Thoughts from Life's Lessons:

Thank God for every sunrise you witness

Strive for goodness for mankind

Give someone a live plant

Learn a new word everyday

Tell someone that they are beautiful

Thank someone "everyday"

Become more positive

Show your enthusiasm for every new day

Care for someone else child as if they were yours

Take time for yourself, just you!

Give time to the elderly

Listen to your love ones

Thank people for being there for you

Forgive yourself

Avoid all negative people

Love yourself

Be kinder daily

Smile more everyday

Everyday find something new about you

Look people directly in the eye when speaking to them

Show more respect

Be responsible for others

Compliment others daily

Be your own hero or shero

Call your love ones often

Honor your obligations to yourself and others

Go to the doctor routinely for checkups

Every chance you get eat dinner with your family

Run bath water for your love one

Buy flowers for your wife or love one, just because

Notes

Notes

Notes

Notes

Notes

Notes

"Author biography"

Mr. Michael is a happily married 60+ year old, who resides in Georgia. He is the proud father of one son and the grandfather of one beautiful girl. He is not a member of the clergy but definitely knows, not just believes in, God Almighty. There is a difference between knowing and believing, and once you realize this universal truth your spirit will soar to untold heights. He felt the compulsion to share with the world the lost art of chivalry and respect for the women of the world. So Enjoy!